W9-BQZ-724

Colourful London

Colourful London

Described by A. N. Court

Jarrold & Sons Ltd, Norwich

Colourful London

No single book can attempt to do justice to the complexity of London, the greatest city of the British Commonwealth. It is the diversity of its appeal, the charm discovered in the most unexpected places and the fascination of its traditions and ceremonies which make London unique among the capitals of the modern world.

The Roman historian Tacitus gives us the first recorded detail of London, which even in the year A.D. 62 was an important market, though not so large as many other Roman settlements. Towards the end of the Roman era London was enclosed by a wall, but little is known of its subsequent history until the reign of King Alfred, who refortified the city against the Danes. The coming of the Normans brought a change in the fortunes of London, for William the Conqueror granted it a charter and began to build the Tower. Westminster Hall was begun by William Rufus, and in 1176 the first London Bridge was built. From about 1190 until the fourteenth century the city was governed by the mayor and aldermen.

At the beginning of the fifteenth century, the period when the benevolent 'Dick' Whittington was four times mayor, the plague first struck London and killed 30,000 people, but the city soon recovered and became extremely prosperous during the sixteenth century. Then, in 1665 and 1666, two catastrophes occurred: the first was another epidemic of plague which killed 100,000 victims, and the other the Great Fire which destroyed practically the whole of the City, including St Paul's Cathedral. Most of London's finest buildings date from the second half of the eighteenth century onwards, and the greatest development of commerce took place in the nineteenth and the present centuries.

This commercial development of the capital makes a fascinating story. Merchant companies had existed in the thirteenth century, and in 1571 Queen Elizabeth I opened the first Royal Exchange. The seventeenth century saw the arrival of French silk weavers and the foundations of the Bank of England, and during the next hundred years trade with distant countries increased considerably. The first London docks were opened in 1802 and the first London railway in 1836. By 1844 there were railways to Birmingham, Southampton and Dover, and the Metropolitan Railway, the first suburban line, was opened in 1863. The twentieth century brought the tube railways, the buses and the trams, and with them the first sign of the traffic problem.

During the Second World War London suffered terribly and there was great destruction, but although three-quarters of all the houses in the capital suffered damage and a third of the City was destroyed, nothing could shake the wonderful spirit of the Londoner. Today the scars are healed; new and more modern buildings have risen from the ruins and London once again greets her visitors with pride.

It is quite impossible in days, or even in weeks, to take stock of all that London has to offer. There is always something new to be discovered, some fresh approach to a familiar scene, some curious piece of history to be investigated. For the visitor who has limited time at his disposal, perhaps the most convenient way of obtaining a general impression of the London scene is for him to take advantage of one of the excellent bus tours organised by London Transport. For those who have more time to be 'out and about' it is preferable to concentrate on each area in turn.

The famous square mile of the City of London is administered as an independent unit, having its own Lord Mayor and Corporation and its own police force. It was here that the Romans built their walled town of Londinium, a few traces of which remain today, and it was here that the medieval guilds established their headquarters. When, after the Great Fire, the City was rebuilt, stone and brick replaced the many mainly wooden medieval houses, and from that time the City gradually became a financial and commercial centre. Today there are within the City boundaries the Bank of England, the Stock Exchange, and headquarters of the principal banking houses, and the chief offices of many insurance companies and import and export businesses. Whenever the Queen makes an official visit to the City the traditional independence of the City of London is symbolised at Temple Bar, where the Lord Mayor presents the Sword of State to Her Majesty as a token of his permission to proceed.

Whereas the City is predominantly concerned with commerce and industry, the West End is largely a residential quarter and a centre of entertainment. The most fashionable district is Mayfair, which lies between Bond Street and Hyde Park. Park Lane, from Marble Arch to Piccadilly, forms the eastern boundary of Hyde Park, a strip of which has been utilised for the doubling of the carriageway. The great houses which formerly faced the park have now been demolished, and in their place rise some of the largest and most exclusive hotels in London.

London's river, the Thames, is of immense importance to the capital, and although it cannot fairly be claimed that the river can compare in beauty with the Seine at Paris, it must be borne in mind that the Thames, with its great docks and wharves, is primarily a commercial waterway, whereas the Seine above Rouen is navigable only to barges. The Thames is born in the Cotswold Hills, where two tiny streams compete for the honour of the title of its source. Its total length is 210 miles, of which more than half is navigable. From Teddington Lock to the Nore the river is tidal, and ocean-going vessels can sail upstream as far as London Bridge. The non-tidal reaches of the river are controlled by the Thames Conservancy Board, but from Teddington to its mouth the river and port installations are the responsibility of the Port of London Authority, a body set up in 1909 which has its headquarters in Trinity Square near the Tower of London. Evidence, in the form of the remains of Roman and British riverside dwellings, points to the fact that at one time the river level was considerably lower than it is today, and until 1831 when the old London Bridge was replaced by the one now being dismantled for shipment to the USA, there were many occasions when the river was frozen over.

The greatest problem facing London today is one of transport: in the first place how to bring an army of workers from the suburbs to the City all within approximately one hour each weekday morning, and how to transport them home in the evening in the same space of time; and secondly how to cope with the ever-increasing volume of traffic on the roads of the capital. Yet in spite of her problems London still remains the principal goal of many thousands of visitors to this country. They come from the four corners of the earth, of every race, creed and colour, and they are made welcome. For they come to a proud city, a city which down the centuries has been threatened many times with destruction but which has always emerged with an unbroken spirit.

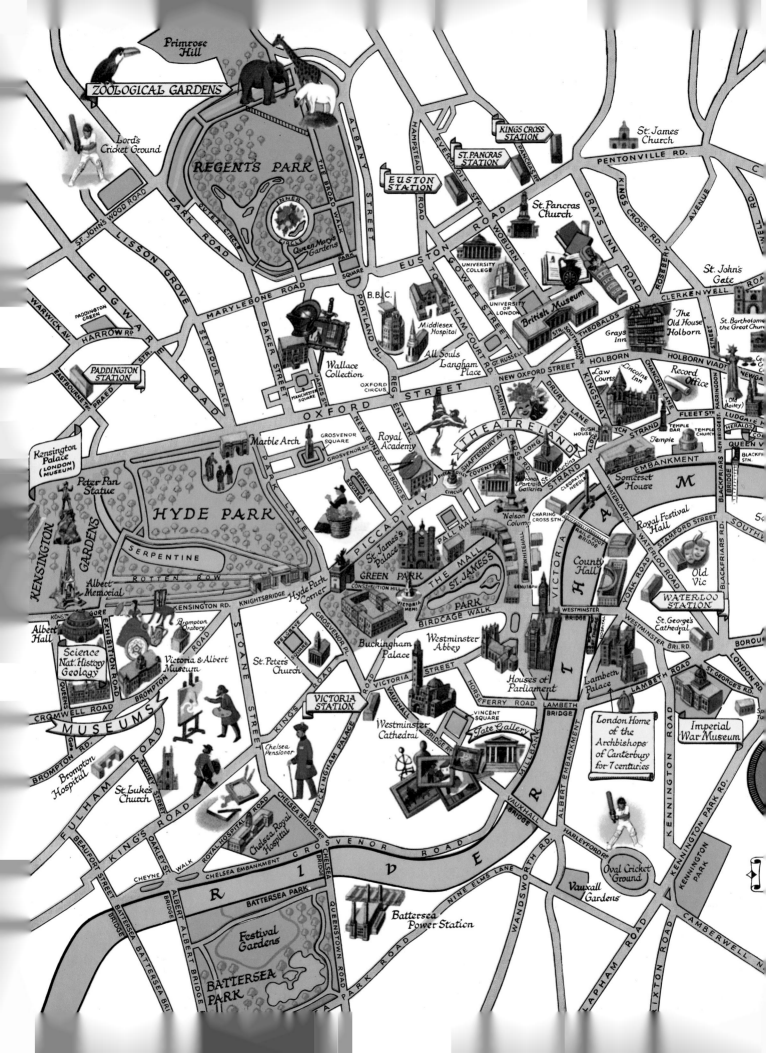

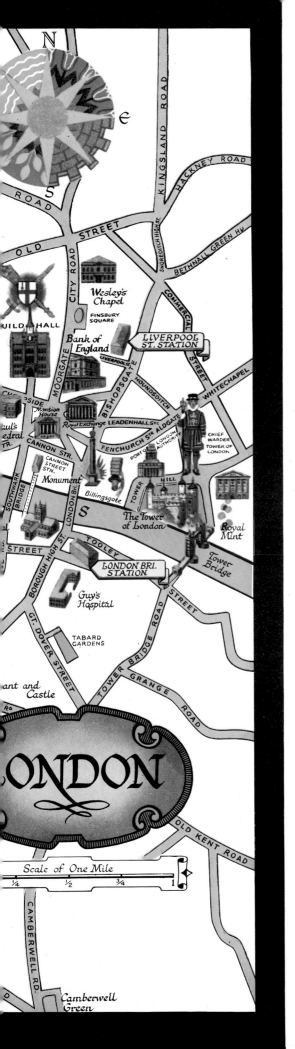

This pictorial map of London covers the area of the metropolis mentioned in this book. It illustrates the most famous landmarks and scenes of pageantry to be found in London, the majority of which are shown in the following pages.

Cette carte illustrée de Londres couvre la surface de la métropole traitée dans ce livre. Elle illustre les plus célebrès etapes et scènes d'apparat que l'on peut voir à Londres; on trouve la majoritè d'entre elles dans les pages suivantes.

Diese Bildkarte Londons umfaßt das ganze Gebiet der Metropol, das in diesem Buch behandelt wird. Sie zeigt die markantesten Punkte und Orte traditioneller Ereignisse in London. Einen Großteil davon finden Sie auf den folgenden Seiten näher illustriert.

The Bank of England (*below, on left*) became nationalised in 1946 and now has few private accounts. Its principal customers are the other banks and the government. Established by Royal Charter in 1694, the Bank of England first carried on its business in borrowed premises, but today it occupies a huge site of nearly four acres opposite the Mansion House. The first permanent building, dating from the 1730s, was considerably enlarged and modified in the latter years of the eighteenth century and the beginning of the nineteenth, to the designs of Sir John Soane. He built the massive outer wall which now conceals an entirely new block of seven storeys, which was completed in 1940. The name 'The Old Lady of Threadneedle Street', sometimes popularly applied to the figure of Britannia on the pediment, was coined by William Cobbett. Between Threadneedle Street and Cornhill stands the Royal Exchange, seen on the right of the photograph below, in front of which stands an equestrian statue of the Duke of Wellington. The first exchange, built by Thomas Gresham in the sixteenth century, was burned down during the Great Fire and its successor met a similar fate in 1838.

The Lord Mayor of London officially resides at the Mansion House, but the seat of the Corporation is Guildhall (*opposite*), and it is here that the Lord Mayor is elected. In Guildhall the City pays tribute to distinguished visitors and to members of the Royal Family, particularly on their return from overseas visits. Guildhall was originally built in the fifteenth century but was modified externally in the eighteenth, and the damage suffered during the last war has now been made good.

Ci-dessus: La Banque d'Angleterre et la Bourse Royale; celle-là établie en 1694 fut rebâtie entre 1930 et 1940
Ci-contre: Guildhall, siège officiel du conseil municipal de Londres.

Oben: Unser Bild zeigt links die Bank of England und rechts die Königliche Börse. *Rechts:* Guildhall, die Versammlungshalle der City of London, auch offizielle Empfangshalle für prominente Gäste.

Tower Bridge (*above*), the most easterly of the many bridges which cross the Thames, may well be called the river gateway of London. It is indeed a gate, for the lower bascules of the bridge can be raised to allow vessels to enter the Pool of London, that stretch of river between Tower Bridge and London Bridge. Tower Bridge was built during the last years of the nineteenth century at a cost, including associated works, of one and a half million pounds.

In the upper photograph on the opposite page Tower Bridge and the Tower of London are seen from the air. For nearly a thousand years the Tower has stood beside the river. William the Conqueror built the massive keep (*prominent in the lower photograph opposite*) which now houses a fine collection of armour. For many years the Tower was a royal residence, and it was also a State prison. The security of the Tower is the responsibility of a military garrison and of the Yeoman Warders or 'Beefeaters' who wear a traditional sixteenth-century uniform.

Ci-contre: Tower Bridge, dont les bascules se lèvent pour permettre aux bateaux de pénétrer dans le Pool, date des dernières années du 19e siècle. *Ci-dessous, en haut:* Une vue aérienne de la Tour de Londres et le Tower Bridge. *Ci-dessous, en bas:* Depuis plus de mille ans des événements historiques ont eu lieu dans la Tour de Londres, autrefois et prison et palais royal. Les « Beefeaters » qui portent toujours leur uniforme de l'époque Tudor (*au centre*) gardent la Tour.

Von allen Themsebrücken Londons ist die Tower Bridge (*ganz links*) am weitesten östlich gelegen. Um auch größeren Schiffen Zufahrt zum Pool von London zu ermöglichen, wird die untere Brücke geöffnet. *Unten:* Ein Luftblick auf den Tower und die Tower Bridge. Der Tower (*ganz unten*) war früher Königspalast und Gefängnis zahlreicher geschichtlicher Persönlichkeiten. Die ,,Beefeaters" (*links*), die noch ihre malerische Tudoruniform tragen, bewachen den Tower.

St Paul's Cathedral (*left*), crowning Ludgate Hill in the historic square mile of the City of London, is one of the most famous landmarks in the capital. It is certainly the third church to stand on the site; in the seventh century there was a Saxon church here which was succeeded by a Norman foundation. This was greatly altered and enlarged in the following centuries, but it fell into disrepair in the seventeenth century and although restoration work was begun under Charles I, the church was almost completely destroyed in the Great Fire of 1666. Yet major calamities often beget great inspiration and the Great Fire was followed by the English Renaissance of which the leading exponent was Sir Christopher Wren. It was Wren who coordinated the rebuilding of St Paul's, the largest Protestant church in England. Wren's design combined dignified Classical external architecture with the normal Gothic internal plan. The dome, perhaps the best known of all London's landmarks, is 365 feet high, and beneath it is the celebrated whispering gallery.

The Central Criminal Court – popularly known as the 'Old Bailey' – seen (*below*) from the Royal Fusiliers Gardens, stands on the site of Newgate Prison, which until the middle of the last century was the principal place of public execution in London. The present building with its copper-covered dome, was opened in 1905 and incorporates part of the former prison.

Ci-contre: La Cathédrale de St Paul, sur le sommet de Ludgate Hill, remplace une ancienne église détruite par le Grand Incendie de 1666. *Ci-dessus:* Le Central Criminal Court, tribunal principal en matière criminelle.

Links: Der Sankt Pauls Dom krönt Ludgate Hill in der Innenstadt. Die frühere Kirche wurde beim Großen Brand im Jahre 1666 zerstört. *Oben:* Old Bailey ist die volkstümliche Bezeichnung für den obersten Gerichtshof.

Situated in the Strand, to the west of Temple Bar, the Royal Courts of Justice (*below*) – the Law Courts, as they are generally called – were erected between 1874 and 1882 to the design of G. E. Street. The vast central hall, over 80 feet in height, is the most notable feature of the building. Civil cases are heard in the various courts, which comprise the Queen's Bench, Appeal, Chancery, Probate, Divorce and Admiralty divisions.

Close to Temple Bar, the boundary of the City of London, two fine churches occupy island sites in the Strand. St Mary-le-Strand (*upper right*) was built in Baroque style in the reign of Queen Anne by James Gibbs; the interior is notable for paintings of the Passion and the Annunciation and for the elaborately carved pulpit. In the background can be seen St Clement Danes, now the official London church of the R.A.F., which was badly damaged during the last war.

Lincoln's Inn Fields (*lower right*), one of the largest residential squares in London, occupies a site to the west of Lincoln's Inn and is notable for the fine seventeenth- and eighteenth-century houses which surround it. In the sixteenth century the fields were used as a place of execution, especially for supporters of the Catholic cause, probably because the Ship Inn in the square had become a refuge for Catholic priests. At the beginning of the seventeenth century Inigo Jones laid out the square as a residential quarter, but almost all of the houses which he designed have disappeared. The present buildings, many of which are occupied by firms of solicitors, are built of red brick and surround a pleasant garden. The Old Curiosity Shop (*far right*) near Lincoln's Inn claims to be the actual premises made famous by Charles Dickens.

Ci-contre: Le Palais de Justice se trouve dans le Strand. *Ci-dessus, à gauche:* Près des limites de la Cité s'élèvent deux églises, situées au milieu de la rue. Du style baroque St Mary le Strand (*au premier plan*) et St Clement Danes (*au fond*), qui a été restaurée comme église de la R.A.F. *Ci-dessus, à droite:* « The Old Curiosity Shop », rendu célèbre par Dickens. *A gauche:* Lincoln's Inn Fields, un des plus grands squares de Londres.

Ganz links: Die Royal Courts of Justice sind für zivile Strafsachen zuständig. *Oben links:* Zwei Kirchen stehen wie Inseln mitten auf dem Strand, einer belebten Hauptstraße Londons, St. Mary le Strand und, im Hintergrund, St. Clement Danes. *Oben rechts:* Der „Old Curiosity Shop" verdankt seine Berühmtheit Charles Dickens. *Links:* Lincolns Inn Fields, einer der ausgedehntesten Plätze Londons.

Il y a quatre écoles à Londres qui confèrent des diplômes de droit. *Ci-dessus:* La résidence du Maître du Middle Temple, près de Fleet street. Dans Middle Temple Lane (*à droite*) les étages des maisons du 17ᵉ siècle surplombent le trottoir. *Ci-contre, en bas:* Le Royal Festival Hall s'élève sur la rive droite de la Tamise. Le premier stade fut achevé en 1951 et le complexe entier en 1965. Du Festival Hall on jouit d'une belle perspective sur la rive gauche avec ses hauts bâtiments.

Es sind vier alte Rechtsschulen in London — die Inns of Court — wo die künftigen Rechtsanwälte studieren. *Oben:* Das Haus des Vorstandsmitglieds des Middle Temple. *Rechts:* Middle Temple Lane ist eine Gasse, wo die oberen Stockwerke der Häuser aus dem 17. Jahrhundert in die Straße hineinragen. *Ganz rechts:* Die Royal Festival Hall auf dem Südufer der Tamise wurde 1951 vollendet. Nebenan stehen die Queen Elizabeth Hall und der Purcell Room. Von diesen Gebäuden aus hat man einen herrlichen Blick auf den Fluß und die Gebäude auf dem linken Ufer.

The City has four Inns of Court where lawyers study for their Bar examinations. They are conducted similarly to the residential colleges of the older universities. Off Fleet Street are the Inner and Middle Temple; Lincoln's Inn is in Chancery Lane and Gray's Inn in Holborn. The Temple possesses one of the five round churches in the country, built in imitation of the Church of the Holy Sepulchre at Jerusalem. The round nave was consecrated in 1185 and the chancel added more than fifty years later. The church and other buildings of the Temple were badly damaged during the Second World War but have been restored. There is documentary evidence that Lincoln's Inn existed in the early years of the fifteenth century and it may well be older still. Gray's Inn has been a school of law for 600 years and although damaged during the Second World War still has its Elizabethan hall. The upper photograph on the opposite page shows the Master's House of the Inner Temple, and the lower view is of Middle Temple Lane which leads from Fleet Street through a Gatehouse designed by Wren. The seventeenth-century buildings flanking the narrow lane have curious overhanging upper storeys.

On the South Bank of the River Thames, situated east of Charing Cross Railway Bridge is a large cultural complex which includes the Royal Festival Hall (*below*). This was built in two stages; the first was completed in time for the Festival of Britain celebrations held in 1951, and the second stage was completed in 1964–5. Designed by Robert Matthew and J. L. Martin the Hall contains an auditorium with seating for over 3,000 people; other accommodation includes exhibition space, meeting rooms and two restaurants. A particular feature of the building is its many windows, mostly overlooking the river and providing fine views of the river and London's skyline. Adjoining the Royal Festival Hall are the Queen Elizabeth Hall, the Purcell Room and the Hayward Art Gallery.

Not far from the Royal Festival Hall the Shell Centre (*below*) towers over the south bank of the Thames. Covering an area of 7 acres it is among the largest company headquarters in Europe; it was designed by Sir Howard Robertson, A.R.A., and built between 1957 and 1962. The centre consists of two massive blocks connected by a tunnel; one of the blocks is L-shaped and the other U-shaped with a tower 351 feet in height and comprising 26 storeys. Visitors are permitted to ascend to the observation gallery on the 25th storey, which at a height of 317 feet gives a splendid view out over London. Not only does the centre house offices for more than 5,000 employees, but it has first-class recreational facilities, including a swimming-pool, a small theatre, restaurants, bars and lounges.

In 1905 the Church of Our Saviour, in the borough of Southwark, became Southwark Cathedral (*opposite*), the second Protestant cathedral of London. The cathedral is believed to occupy the site of a nunnery of the ninth century, and there may well have been a Roman temple here, as Roman tiles were found during excavation and these have been placed in the choir aisle. In 1106 a priory of Augustinian Canons was founded here and a Norman church was built. This Priory Church of St Mary Overie was unfortunately almost completely burned down in 1212. A Gothic church was built in about 1220 incorporating the remains of the Norman church, and a Norman arch discovered during later restoration is still to be seen in the Harvard Chapel, a memorial to the founder of the American university. After the Priory was dissolved, the Priory Church became in 1540 the Parish Church of St Saviour, Southwark. In 1838 the nave of this medieval church largely collapsed and in 1890 was reconstructed to the design of Sir Arthur Blomfield, as the first step towards the church being created Southwark Cathedral. Although a cathedral, St Saviour's has also remained a parish church, serving the needs of its district as well as the diocese. The Choir and the Lady Chapel are considered to be among the finest Gothic architecture in London.

Ci-contre: L'église de notre Sauveur, la cathédrale de Southwark; une partie du bâtiment date du 13e siècle. *Ci-dessus:* Perspective du centre Shell sur la rive droite de la Tamise.

Rechts: Die Southwark Cathedral wurde auf den Fundamenten einer normannischen Kirche erbaut. Der älteste Teil des erhaltenen Bauwerks stammt aus dem Jahre 1207. *Oben:* Ein Blick auf das Shell Centre auf dem Südufer.

Ci-dessus: L'Embankment, sur la rive gauche de la Tamise. Le Shell Building, éclairé la nuit, a l'horloge publique la plus grande de Londres. *Ci-dessous:* La Tamise, vue d'aval. Waterloo Bridge au premier plan est un des plus élégants des nombreux ponts qui enjambent le fleuve. *Ci-contre:* La Tamise, vue d'amont.

Oben: Die Embankment (Ufereinfassung) mit dem beleuchteten Shellgebäude; die Uhr ist die größte öffentliche Uhr Londons. *Unten:* Die Themse, stromabwärts. Waterloo Bridge im Vordergrund ist eine der schönsten Brücken, die den Strom überspannen. *Rechts:* Die Themse, stromaufwärts.

From time to time various schemes have been carried out with the object of improving London's riverside. One such project was the construction of the Victoria Embankment, extending from Westminster to Blackfriars, which was completed in 1870 and opened by the Prince of Wales. In the view below, the river is seen stretching away westwards to Westminster and beyond. Hungerford Bridge, in the foreground, carries the railway from Charing Cross. Beyond it Westminster and Lambeth Bridges span the river. The obelisk on the river bank is 'Cleopatra's Needle', an ancient Egyptian monument which about 3500 years ago stood in front of the temple of the sun at Heliopolis. It was removed to Alexandria by Augustus Cæsar and after many vicissitudes its final journey began in 1877, when a tug towed the monument, encased in a metal cylinder, away from the Egyptian port. The tug, unfortunately, sank in the Bay of Biscay, but the cylinder and its historic burden were rescued and the 'needle' at last arrived in London and was erected on the Embankment in 1878.

The upper photograph on the opposite page shows the Victoria Embankment at night, with Shell-Mex House floodlit. This building boasts the largest public clock in London. Behind the trees on the right of the picture stands the Savoy, one of the best known of London's hotels. In the lower photograph the river stretches away eastwards towards the City. In the foreground is Waterloo Bridge, rebuilt during the thirties, one of the most attractive of the bridges across the river. In the distance the dome of St Paul's is clearly visible to the left of Blackfriar's Bridge. One of the best ways of getting to know London's river is to make use of the service of water-buses which ply in summer between Richmond and Greenwich.

Ci-contre: Une vue générale sur Trafalgar Square qui est dominé par l'énorme colonne, surmontée d'une statue de Lord Nelson. Aux coins du socle reposent les quatre lions de Landseer. *Ci-dessus, à gauche:* A Noël la place est ornée d'un sapin illuminé. *Ci-dessus, à droite:* L'église de St Martin-in-the-Fields se trouve au coin nord-est de la place. *A droite:* Un visiteur donne à manger aux nombreux pigeons qui fréquentent la place.

Ganz rechts: Ein Blick auf Trafalgar Square; ein 16-Fuß hohes Standbild von Lord Nelson krönt die auffallende Säule. Um den Sockel liegen Landseers vier Steinlöwen. *Oben links:* Zur Weihnachtszeit leuchtet ein riesengroßer Tannenbaum hervor. *Oben rechts:* Die berühmte St. Martin's-in-the-Fields Kirche im nordöstlichen Winkel des Platzes. *Rechts:* Trafalgar Square zieht Tausende von Besuchern an, die die Tauben gern füttern.

Sooner or later every visitor finds his or her way to Trafalgar Square, a general view of which appears below. Surmounting the imposing column, a copy of one of the Corinthian columns in the Temple of Mars at Rome, is the 17-foot-high statue of Lord Nelson. The total height of the monument is over 170 feet. On the pedestal are bronze reliefs representing Nelson's most famous victories. The bronze lions at the corners of the pedestal are the work of Landseer.

The whole of the northern side of Trafalgar Square is taken up by the façade of the National Gallery. Adjoining is the National Portrait Gallery containing a collection of portraits and sculptures of eminent British men and women from the sixteenth century onwards. The north-east corner of the square is occupied by the well-known Church of St Martin-in-the-Fields (*upper left*). The building was designed by James Gibbs, who is best remembered for his work at King's College, Cambridge. It stands on the site of an earlier church where Francis Bacon and Charles II were both baptised. Some of the earliest broadcast religious services came from St Martin's, and the crypt has for many years been kept open at night as a refuge for the destitute.

At Christmas Trafalgar Square is decorated by a huge fir tree (*far left*) presented by the Norwegian government, but the real attraction of the square is the pigeons (*lower left*). Huge flocks of these birds, seemingly with insatiable appetites, people the square, and are so very tame that they will readily alight on an outstretched arm or even an unsuspecting head.

The National Gallery (*below*) houses one of the finest collections of European art from the thirteenth century onwards. The central part of the building dates from 1838 and was designed by William Wilkins, who incorporated into his Classical portico the columns from Carlton House which had been pulled down. The gallery was enlarged in the middle of the nineteenth century and since the end of the last war has been extensively reconstructed. Of the numerous paintings, the collection of the Italian School is considered to be the finest in the country. To the rear of the gallery, in St Martin's Place, stands the National Portrait Gallery, which was opened in 1896. It contains a comprehensive collection of portraits of British men and women from the sixteenth century.

Piccadilly Circus (*upper right*) has often been called the hub of the Commonwealth, and it is certainly one of the busiest junctions in the West End. Beneath the roadway lies one of the main interchange stations of London's underground railway network. In the centre of the circus stands the well-known statue of Eros, a memorial to one of London's greatest philanthropists, the seventh Earl of Shaftesbury.

Coventry Street leads from Piccadilly Circus towards Leicester Square (*lower right*), which was laid out in the seventeenth century and was once notorious as a venue for duellists. Its fashionable residences have long since disappeared, but the square retains something of the leisurely air of a bygone age. In the centre of the garden is a bust of William Shakespeare, a copy of the one to be seen in Westminster Abbey, and at the four corners are busts of former residents: Isaac Newton, Joshua Reynolds, William Hogarth and John Hunter.

The whole of the area around Piccadilly Circus and Leicester Square forms the heart of London's West End. Here are to be found many of the principal theatres and cinemas and a host of restaurants and clubs. At night the district is a blaze of light, (*centre right*).

Ci-contre: Les Galeries Nationales de la Peinture occupent tout le côté nord de Trafalgar Square. On y trouve les principales collections de l'Angleterre. Ci-dessus: Piccadilly Circus s'appelle le centre du Commonwealth. Au milieu s'élève la statue d'Eros au-dessous de laquelle se trouve une des stations les plus mouvementées du Métro de Londres. A gauche, en haut: Ce quartier est éclairé la nuit par mille réclames à néon. A gauche, en bas: Leicester Square est située au milieu du quartier le plus gai de la capitale. La place est entourée de restaurants, de cinémas et de théâtres. Le jardin fut disposé au cours du 17e siècle.

Links: Die Nationalgalerie und die Nationalporträtgalerie auf der Nordseite des Trafalgar Square sind Londons bedeutendste Gemäldegalerien, wo vortreffliche Sammlungen zu sehen sind. Oben: Zu den belebtesten Verkehrszentren gehört zweifellos Piccadilly Circus. Mitten auf dem Platz erhebt sich die Statue von Eros, und unten liegt eine der wichtigsten Stationen der Untergrundbahn. Links oben: Am Abend leuchten zahlreiche Lichtreklamen auf. Links unten: Leicester Square befindet sich im belebtesten Stadtviertel. Theater, Kinos und Restaurants umgeben den Platz, der im 17. Jahrhundert angelegt wurde.

Many of London's largest stores are situated in Oxford Street (*below*) and Regent Street which intersect at Oxford Circus. A little to the north of the circus stands Broadcasting House, the headquarters of the BBC. The great shops of the West End, one of which boasts that it can supply anything from a pin to an elephant, attract many thousands of visitors every year. At Christmas time Oxford Street and Regent Street are gay with an elaborate scheme of illuminated decorations (*lower right*). For many years these have been designed and made by a small firm in Suffolk, specialising in this craft, and in subsequent years the illuminations are acquired by other towns for their own festivities.

The tallest building in the capital, and indeed in Britain, is the Post Office Tower (*far right*) which was opened to the public in May 1966, although it had been operational for some seven months before that date. The tower, including its mast, has a total height of 625 feet and provides micro-wave links which can be beamed to all parts of the country. The height of the tower was necessary in order that the signals would have an uninterrupted path clear of all obstructions. Approximately 150,000 simultaneous circuits are provided for telephone, television and computer services, each carrier wave being able to carry up to 2700 telephone calls. The mast at the top of the tower also carries meteorological equipment which is of considerable value in the preparation of weather forecasts. In addition to its primary function as a telecommunications centre, the tower provides a new and exciting addition to the sights of London. Two lifts convey visitors at 1000 feet a minute to three observation platforms, the uppermost of which is almost 500 feet high. Above them is a restaurant which revolves slowly around the central part of the tower and offers the finest views of London. London's Post Office Tower will be the highest of a series which will ultimately cover the whole of the British Isles, and the radio links provided will largely obviate the need for expensive cables.

Beaucoup des grands magasins de Londres sont situés dans Oxford Street (*ci-dessous, à gauche*) et Regent Street qui se croisent à Oxford Circus. A Noël des milliers de visiteurs viennent dans ce quartier pour admirer les belles illuminations (*ci-dessous, à droite*). *A droite:* La Post Office Tower est le centre de télécommunication le plus moderne de l'Angleterre. Ouverte au publique en mai 1966, elle est le plus haut édifice de Londres. La tour est haute de plus de 190 mètres et près du sommet se trouve un restaurant tournant. Il y a trois plates-formes d'observation, dont la plus élevée a une hauteur de 150 mètres.

Viele der größten Warenhäuser befinden sich in der Regent Street und in der Oxford Street (*links*), die sich am Oxford Circus kreuzen. In diesen Kaufhäusern soll man alles von einem Elefanten bis zu einer Stecknadel kaufen können. Zur Weihnachtszeit kommen Tausende von Besuchern zu diesen beiden Hauptstraßen, um die festliche Beleuchtung zu bewundern (*unten — Regent Street*). *Rechts:* Der neue Postturm ist nicht nur das höchste Gebäude Londons sondern auch eine der modernsten Fernverbindungszentralen in England. Der Turm hat ein Drehrestaurant und drei Aussichtsplattformen.

The broad tree-lined thoroughfare of the Mall, along which so many historic processions have passed, leads from Buckingham Palace to Trafalgar Square. At the latter end, and adjoining the Admiralty of which it forms part, stands the impressively proportioned Admiralty Arch (*below*), designed by Sir Aston Webb and completed in 1911 as part of the national memorial to Queen Victoria. On the north side of the Mall is St James's Palace, built by Henry VIII on the site of a hospital for leprous maidens. Of the sixteenth-century palace there remain the Gatehouse, part of the Chapel and the Audience Chamber. When Whitehall Palace was destroyed by fire, St James's was used as the London residence of the Court until Queen Victoria moved into Buckingham Palace. St James's, however, is still the official Court and all ambassadors are accredited to it.

Whitehall (*upper right*), leading from Trafalgar Square to the Houses of Parliament at Westminster, is flanked by many large administrative buildings. Its name perpetuates the former Palace of Whitehall which stood here until the eighteenth century and which was the principal centre of Court life in Tudor and Stuart times. Of the palace, where Henry VIII died and where Elizabeth I entertained, there remains only the Banqueting Hall, in front of which Charles I was executed. In Downing Street, a turning off Whitehall, is situated the most famous house in London – No. 10 – the official residence of the Prime Minister. Next door at No. 11 the Chancellor of the Exchequer has his official residence. Close at hand, in the centre of Whitehall, stands the Cenotaph (*lower right*), the memorial to the fallen of both world wars. It was designed by Sir Edward Lutyens and unveiled on 11 November 1920. Every November on Armistice Sunday a service is held at the Cenotaph which is attended by the Queen and other members of the Royal family.

Ci-contre: A l'extrémité est du Mall s'élève Admiralty Arch qui fut construite en 1911 pour faire partie du monument national à la reine Victoria. Depuis Trafalgar Square on descend Whitehall (*ci-dessus*) pour arriver au Parlement à Westminster. Dans la rue se dressent plusieurs bâtiments de l'administration britannique. La demeure du Premier Ministre à 10 Downing Street est près du Cénotaph (*à gauche*), monument aux morts des deux guerres mondiales. Le Monument, œuvre de Lutyens, fut consacré le 11 novembre 1920.

Ganz links: Admiralty Arch ist ein Teil des Nationaldenkmals, das 1911 für die Königin Victoria fertiggestellt wurde. *Oben:* Von zahlreichen Verwaltungsgebäuden gesäumt, führt Whitehall, eine breite Hauptstraße, vom Trafalgar Square aus zu den Parlamentsgebäuden in Westminster. No. 10 Downing Street in der Nähe von Whitehall ist der Amtssitz des Premierministers und ist wohl das berühmteste Haus in London. *Links:* Das Zenotaph, ein Ehrendenkmal dür die Gefallenen beider Weltkriege, wurde am 11. November 1920 eingeweiht.

Units of the Brigade of Guards are normally stationed in London. The Brigade consists of the Household Cavalry and the five regiments of Foot Guards. The former comprises the Life Guards and the Royal Horse Guards – the 'Blues' – and their magnificent horses and accoutrements are a constant source of wonder and admiration. The Household Cavalry provides a sovereign's escort for the Queen and visiting rulers and a captain's escort for other distinguished people. The two regiments of the Household Cavalry are easily distinguished: the Life Guards wear red tunics and have white plumes in their helmets; the tunics of the Royal Horse Guards are blue and their plumes red. The history of these two mounted regiments is a fascinating one, its most colourful period occurring in the days of the Stuarts. In 1685 the Life Guards of Horse were formed and two years later the Royal Regiment of Horse. Almost exactly a century later, in 1788, the Life Guards were reorganised into the first and second Regiments and the Royal Horse Guards Blue became the Royal Horse Guards ('the Blues') in 1819. The two regiments of Life Guards were amalgamated in 1922.

Between Whitehall and St James's Park lies Horse Guards, once a guard-house for the royal palace of Whitehall. One of the most popular sights in London is the Changing of the Mounted Guard in the forecourt of the former palace (*below*). The sentries, resplendent in their full-dress uniforms on their magnificent perfectly groomed horses, are an attraction which never fails to draw a large number of sightseers. At the conclusion of the ceremony two mounted sentries are posted at the entrance facing Whitehall (*left*). Behind the forecourt a passage leads to the extensive open space known as Horse Guards Parade.

Ci-contre: une sentinelle montée des Gardes du Corps. La tenue magnifique de ces militaires fait l'admiration de tout le monde. *Ci-dessus:* La relève de la garde dans la cour de Horse Guards.

Links: Ein berittener Leibgardist in farbenprächtiger Uniform hält Wache gegenüber dem ehemaligen Whitehall Palast. *Oben:* Die Wachablösung der Horse Guards ist für alle ein beliebtes Schauspiel.

In the modern age, when the pursuit of the practical and expedient is tending towards the suppression of tradition, it is perhaps surprising to find that, of all the great cities of the world, London maintains a considerable number of ceremonies which bring colour and pageantry to the capital. There was, of course, a time when the presence of troops in London was a necessity for the security of the Crown, but happily this situation no longer pertains, and Londoners and visitors see the military principally on ceremonial occasions.

The most colourful of these military parades is the ceremony of Trooping the Colour which takes place every year in June on Horse Guards Parade, in celebration of the official birthday of the sovereign. The military formations taking part are the Household Cavalry and the Brigade of Guards, each battalion of the latter having in turn the honour of 'trooping' its own colour. The ceremony has its origin in the time when the battle standard was the rallying point for troops in the field. The three photographs on these pages reveal something of the splendour of the ceremony. In the lower photograph right the Queen, followed by other members of her family and escorted by a sovereign's escort of the Household Cavalry, is seen arriving at Horse Guards; the view above shows Her Majesty crossing the parade ground to take her place at the saluting base.

The ceremony of Trooping the Colour is a complicated one, necessitating careful rehearsal and precise timing. The climax comes with a combined march-past, first in slow and then in quick time, when the colour is carried at the head of the marching troops and dipped in salute to the sovereign. Finally the Queen leads her Guards from the parade ground.

La Parade du Drapeau (Trooping the Colour) a lieu tous les ans au mois de juin à Horse Guards Parade en l'honneur de l'anniversaire officiel de la Reine. Chaque régiment de la Brigade of Guards a l'honneur à tour de rôle de faire parade de son drapeau devant Sa Majesté. *Ci-contre:* La Household Cavalry fait une conversion autour des Gardes à Pied. *Ci-dessus:* Les Gardes à Pied arrivent pour la cérémonie. *A gauche:* La Reine, montée en amazone, suivie d'autres membres de la famille royale, arrive à Horse Guards Parade, pour rendre le salut militaire. A la fin de la cérémonie la Reine mène ses troupes de la place.

Zur offiziellen Geburtstagsfeier des Staatsoberhauptes veranstaltet man jedes Jahr im Monat Juni die traditionelle Fahnenparade (Trooping the Colour). Der Reihe nach hat jedes Regiment der Brigade of Guards die Ehre, mit seiner eigenen Fahne vor der Königin Parade zu halten. *Ganz links:* Die berittene Leibgarde vollführt eine Schwenkung um die strammstehenden Foot Guards. *Links:* Die Königin, gefolgt von Mitgliedern des Königshauses, ist gerade bei den Horse Guards eingetroffen. Sie reitet über den Paradeplatz zu dem Standort, von wo aus sie die Parade abnehmen wird. *Oben:* Die Foot Guards marschieren nach dem Paradeplatz.

A droite et ci-dessous: Le Parlement qui date du 19e siècle renferme une partie de l'ancien Palais de Westminster. La Chambre de Communes, bombardée en 1941, a été rebâti. Au premier plan ou voit Westminster Bridge. *Ci-contre:* County Hall, conseil municipal du comité du Londres est situé presque en face du Parlement. La nuit plusieurs bâtiments importants de Londres, tels que County Hall et le Parlement sont illuminés par projecteurs.

Rechts und unten: Die Parlamentsgebäude in London sind der Sitz der Regierung Groß-Britanniens. Sie wurden im vorigen Jahrhundert errichtet und schließen einen Teil des mittelalterlichen Westminsterpalasts ein. Das Unterhaus wurde 1941 im Krieg zerstört und ist wiederaufgebaut worden. *Ganz rechts:* County Hall, wo der Londonergrafschaftsrat tagt. Nachts werden zahlreiche Gebäude Londons angestrahlt.

Many of London's most notable buildings are floodlit during the summer months, and form especially attractive subjects for photographers. Below is a view of County Hall, the headquarters of the Greater London Council, which occupies a prominent position on the south bank of the Thames almost opposite the Houses of Parliament. The foundation stone was laid by King George V in 1912. He opened the first part some ten years later, but the building was not finally completed until 1933. The interior is notable for the fine use made of various coloured marble. All the seating in the Council Chamber is of oak, but the seats for the chairman and his deputies are made of ancient bog-wood, found during excavation at Charing Cross.

The upper photograph opposite is a fine view of the Houses of Parliament from County Hall. The river frontage has a length of 870 feet. On the left rises the Victoria Tower, the highest of the three. Through the archway at the foot of this tower the sovereign passes on the occasion of a Royal opening of Parliament. The Union Jack flies from the Victoria Tower whenever Parliament is in session, and at night a light in the Clock Tower at the other end of the building gives the same information. The lower photograph opposite shows the Houses of Parliament from a similar angle but at night. In the foreground we see Westminster Bridge, one of the finest bridges in Europe. This was originally constructed in the middle of the eighteenth century, but was replaced by the present structure, opened in 1862. The massive statue of Boadicea and her chariot at its western end was designed by Thomas Thornycroft and placed here at the beginning of this century.

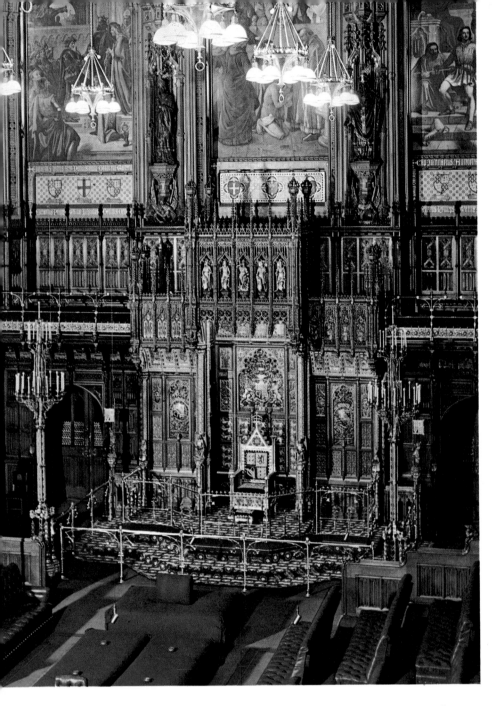

Ci-dessus: L'intérieur de la Chambre des Lords dans le Parlement. Devant le trône se trouve le Woolsack, siège du Lord Chancelier. *A droite:* le clocher de « Big Ben », célèbre dans le monde entier. *Ci-contre:* Le Parlement vu de Old Palace Yard. Au premier plan se dresse le monument à la mémoire du Roi Georges V qui fut dévoilé par son successeur en 1947. A gauche on voit une partie de l'Abbaye de Westminster et au fond Westminster Hall.

Oben: Das Innere des Oberhauses (House of Lords). Vor dem Thron sieht man den Woolsack, den Sitz des Lord Chancellor. *Rechts:* der Uhrturm mit der weltberühmten Uhr „Big Ben". *Ganz rechts:* Die Parlamentsgebäude, von Old Palace Yard ausgesehen. Im Vordergrund steht das Denkmal für den König Georg V., das im Jahre 1947 von seinem Nachfolger entschleiert wurde. Im Hintergrund sieht man einen Teil der Westminster Hall.

The Houses of Parliament were completed a century ago on the site of the old Palace of Westminster, of which nothing remains but Westminster Hall, the Jewel Tower and parts of St Stephen's Chapel which were incorporated into the present building. The architecture is late Gothic and the building extends over eight acres.

The House of Lords (*far left*) is an ornately furnished chamber with fine carving and frescoes, some depicting incidents in English history, others symbolic of virtues. The peers' benches are covered in red leather, the same colour as that of the Woolsack, the traditional seat of the Lord Chancellor. Behind the Woolsack stands the Throne from which the sovereign ceremonially opens each session of Parliament. The present House of Commons is new, for the old chamber was destroyed by enemy action in 1941. Although it was rebuilt in the same style as before, the opportunity was taken to increase the number of seats in the galleries and to modernise the fittings. At its entrance stands the Churchill Arch, constructed from stone salvaged from the original chamber. The photograph on the left is of the Clock Tower of the Houses of Parliament which contains the hour bell, famous the world over as Big Ben. The Clock Tower is over 300 feet in height and each of the four clock-faces has a diameter of over 22 feet.

Below is a view of the Parliament buildings from Old Palace Yard. In the foreground stands the National Memorial to King George V which was unveiled by his successor in 1947. On the left is a portion of the Abbey and, on the far side of the roadway, Westminster Hall. This, the oldest part of Parliament, was begun at the end of the eleventh century in the reign of William II. It was refashioned and enlarged by subsequent monarchs, notably Richard II who caused it to receive its fine oak roof at the end of the fourteenth century. Many famous trials have been held in this historic hall, including those of Guy Fawkes, Charles I and Warren Hastings. It was in Westminster Hall that the bodies of Edward VII, George V and George VI lay in state.

Between the Houses of Parliament and Lambeth Bridge are Victoria Tower Gardens which contain Rodin's famous sculpture *The Burghers of Calais* and the Suffragettes Memorial. At Lambeth Bridge we join Millbank, seen (*right*) from the Albert Embankment. The 387-foot-high tower block, known as the Millbank Tower, or Vickers House, was until comparatively recently the tallest of the post-war office blocks in London. In the foreground of the photograph is one of the river-stations of the London Fire Brigade, the headquarters of which are on the far side of the Albert Embankment. The present brigade was formed in 1965 to serve the Greater London Council and incorporates the former London service together with most of the former Middlesex, Croydon and East and West Ham brigades. The river-stations can deal speedily not only with fires occurring in river craft, but also with fires in buildings on the river banks. The police, too, has a special river-based force, the Thames Division of the Metropolitan Police. This is the successor to an organisation set up at the end of the eighteenth century by London merchants, whose cargoes and ships were often attacked by thieves. The division has five police-stations, one of which is actually on the river.

Below is a view of the Houses of Parliament from the Albert Embankment by night. Near the eastern end of the bridge stands Lambeth Palace, the London residence of the Archbishop of Canterbury. Although the Palace was badly damaged during the war, it has been restored, and the oldest parts of the building include the late fifteenth-century gatehouse and the Lollards Tower.

Ci-dessus: La nuit on jouit d'une belle perspective de Westminster avec Lambeth Bridge au premier plan; au loin — Westminster Bridge et la tour de Big Ben. *Ci-contre:* Millbank Tower, située sur la rive gauche de la Tamise.

Oben: Unser Bild zeigt zwei berühmte Brücken in Westminster; Lambeth Bridge und Westminster Bridge. *Rechts:* Eines der vielen Wahrzeichen Londons, die nach dem zweiten Weltkrieg entstanden sind: Millbank Tower.

Westminster Abbey, as we know it today, dates largely from the time of Henry VII, and it is one of the finest examples of Early English architecture in the country. The Abbey, however, had been founded by Edward the Confessor in 1050 and it remained a Benedictine monastery until the Dissolution. Edward based his church on the Abbey of Jumièges in Normandy, and it was in the Confessor's church that William the Conqueror was crowned King of England. Since that time the coronation of every English sovereign, except Edward V and Edward VIII, has taken place in the Abbey. The rebuilding of the Abbey, which was begun by Henry III, lasted for nearly 300 years. The Norman work of the nave, which had been left standing by Henry III, was rebuilt in the late fourteenth century, and the chantries of Henry V and Henry VI were added in succeeding centuries. The imposing west towers and the façade were not built until the first half of the eighteenth century.

The photograph below gives a good idea of the scale and proportions of Westminster Abbey, seen from Dean's Yard. The upper photographs opposite are (*on the left*) the west towers and (*on the right*) a view of the choir. The lower photograph is of the Shrine of Edward the Confessor which was erected in 1269 some 200 years after his death. The abbey is a veritable treasure-house of British history, for not only is it the resting-place of monarchs, but it contains memorials and tombs of many of those who have brought honour to their country. Among the treasures of the Abbey are the Coronation Chair, made for the Confessor, and the Stone of Scone, on which the Scottish kings were once crowned. One grave is honoured above all others – that of the unknown warrior, the representative of the fallen of the First World War.

Ci-contre: L'Abbaye de Westminster, où a lieu depuis 1066 le couronnement de presque tous les souverains britanniques. L'Abbaye fut fondée en 1050 par Édouard le Confesseur et pendant le règne d'Henri III la reconstruction commença, une tâche qui dura presque 300 années. *Ci-dessus, à gauche:* Les deux tours et la façade ouest de l'Abbaye. *Ci-dessus à droite:* Perspective du chœur. L'Abbaye a beaucoup de trésors, y compris le tombeau d'Édouard le Confesseur (*à gauche*) et celui du Soldat Inconnu.

Ganz links: Ein Blick auf die Abtei von Westminster, von Dean's Yard ausgesehen. Die Abtei wurde im Jahre 1050 von Edward dem Bekenner gegründet; unter der Regierung Henrichs des Dritten wurde die Wiederherstellung begonnen, und diese Arbeit dauerte fast 300 Jahre. *Oben links:* Die Westtürme und die Fassade sind der neueste Teil des Gebäudes. *Oben rechts:* Ein Blick auf den Chor. *Links:* Der Schrein von Edward dem Bekenner, der von dem 13. Jahrhundert stammt.

Westminster Cathedral (*left*) is the principal Roman Catholic church in England. Although its architecture is Early Byzantine in style, it is nevertheless a modern building, having been begun in 1895 and consecrated 1910. The cathedral is very large and its nave is the widest in England. The interior is embellished with striking marble and mosaic. Of particular note are the exquisitely carved marble pillars, each of which is different from the others, and the huge crucifix, weighing two tons, at the Sanctuary entrance. Externally the most prominent feature of the building is the campanile (273 feet high), surmounted by an 11-foot-high cross.

The Tate Gallery (*below*) in Millbank is named after Sir Henry Tate who gave it to the nation. The building was designed by Sidney Smith and opened by King Edward VII in 1897, when he was Prince of Wales. Originally it was built to house a National Collection of British Painting, but it was later enlarged and now contains, in addition to some 4000 British paintings, collections of modern foreign works, both of painting and of sculpture. Among the British artists represented are Hogarth, Gainsborough, Turner, Reynolds, Millais, Whistler, John, and Sutherland.

La Tate Galerie dans Millbank (*ci-dessus*) a une belle collection de peintures, dont la plupart sont par des artistes britanniques. La cathédrale de Westminster (*ci-contre*) est la principale église catholique d'Angleterre.

Die Tate Gallery (*oben*) enthält eine prächtige Gemäldesammlung von britischen Malern. Die Kathedrale von Westminster (*links*) ist die bedeutendste katholische Kirche Englands.

Ci-dessus: St James's Park s'étend de Buckingham Palace jusqu'à Whitehall. C'est à l'époque de Charles II que le parc fut disposé pour ressembler au parc de Versailles. Sous le règne de Georges IV il fut transformé dans le style anglais. Sa particularité la plus intéressante est un petit lac charmant. *A droite:* St James's Park au printemps, quand les tulipes paraissent. *Ci-contre:* Des visiteurs donnent à manger aux oiseaux aquatiques qui peuplent le lac.

Oben: St. James's Park dehnt sich vom Buckingham Palast bis zu Whitehall. Unter der Regierung Karls des Zweiten wurde der Park angelegt, um dem Park zu Versailles ähnlich zu sein. In der Zeit Georgs des Vierten wurde die Anlage geändert und jetzt sieht der Park vollkommen englisch aus. *Rechts:* Im Frühling sind die Tulpen besonders schön. *Ganz rechts:* Im Park befindet sich ein kleiner reizender See, den allerlei Wasservögel bevölkern. Es macht den Besuchern Spaß, sie zu füttern.

It was a happy circumstance that when Henry VIII acquired the site for St James's Palace he added also the grounds owned by the hospital, which became St James's Park. At one time the park was the most fashionable promenade in London, and Charles II in particular took a great interest in it, not only supervising its layout but establishing an aviary for waterfowl. In 1827 the park was re-modelled by Nash who combined the several existing ponds into one ornamental lake and built an attractive suspension bridge. Today the park is a favourite rendezvous of those who work in the many offices in the vicinity. Green Park, which is bounded on the south by Constitution Hill and the Mall and on the north by Piccadilly, is really a continuation of St James's Park, and before its area was reduced in the reign of George III it was sometimes known as Upper St James's Park. On the eastern side is a fine path, known as 'Queen's Walk', reputed to be named after Queen Caroline, the wife of George II. At the western end of the park, at the junction of Piccadilly and Constitution Hill, stands the Wellington – or Green Park – Arch. This was formerly opposite the main entrance of Hyde Park and was surmounted by an equestrian statue of the Duke of Wellington, but on its removal in 1912 to its present position the statue was replaced by the figure of Peace alighting on a chariot of war.

The upper photograph on the opposite page shows part of St James's Park in autumn, when the colour of the foliage is at its most attractive. In contrast, the lower photograph opposite was taken earlier in the year, when the carefully tended beds are ablaze with tulips and other spring flowers. The monument commemorates the men of the Guards Division who lost their lives during the world wars, and in the background is the façade of Horse Guards. In the view below, visitors are seen feeding the pigeons and waterfowl at the side of the attractive lake. Part of the front of Buckingham Palace can be seen in the distance.

Pageantry takes many forms, from a simple guard-duty to an elaborate ceremony such as a coronation or a royal wedding. Functions such as the latter do not, it is true, take place very often, but there are daily ceremonies to be seen in various parts of London. At the royal palaces and in Whitehall guard-mounting is carried out every day, and each evening a detachment of one officer and fifteen men establishes a guard at the Bank of England. This is a practice dating from 1780, when the Bank was attacked during the Gordon Riots. The posting of a relief sentry is a piece of traditional ceremonial which never fails to arouse the interest of the visitor.

The Mall is the capital's best-known ceremonial road, and the crowds who throng the railings of Buckingham Palace are frequently rewarded by the spectacle of a detachment of the Brigade of Guards marching to and from the Palace. Each of the regiments of Foot Guards – Grenadier, Cold-stream, Welsh, Irish, and Scots Guards – has a proud distinguished record in past campaigns. Each regiment of the Brigade of Guards has its military band and these perform not only on ceremonial occasions in London but have frequent engagements at sporting and other occasions in every part of the country and sometimes abroad. Nor must it be forgotten that every guardsman is a fully trained soldier, ready for immediate service wherever he may be required. The photograph on the opposite page shows a detachment of Life Guards in the Mall, while below a band of Foot Guards makes its majestic way along this famous thoroughfare.

Ci-contre: Un détachement de Life Guards, montés sur leurs chevaux magnifiques quitte le Palais, à l'occasion de la répétition d'une cérémonie. *Ci-dessus:* La musique d'un régiment de la Garde à l'entrée du Palais.

Links: Eine Abteilung Life Guards auf ihren stattlichen Rossen verläßt den Palast bei einer Feierprobe. *Oben:* Die Musik der Foot Guards in der Nähe des Palasts.

The Royal Standard flying over Buckingham Palace (*below*) is the sign that the Queen is in residence. This eighteenth-century house was purchased by George III in 1762, rebuilt later by Nash, and since 1837 it has been continuously used as the official London residence of the sovereign. Facing the Palace at the end of the broad Mall stands the statue of Queen Victoria. The white marble memorial, surmounted by the winged figure of 'Victory', was unveiled in 1911. The imposing stone façade of the palace was added by Sir Aston Webb in 1913. Buckingham Palace is the private home of the Royal Family, and as such is never on view to the public. Many of the rooms are of immense size and contain a magnificent collection of paintings and other works of art; the gardens extend over forty acres.

Most of the world's capitals have their Hilton Hotel, and London is no exception. The London Hilton (*right*), a modern luxury hotel, stands at the southern end of Park Lane facing Hyde Park. Near by are two other leading hotels, the Dorchester and Grosvenor House.

The open spaces of London provide a welcome contrast to the great built-up areas. The largest is Hyde Park (*lower right*), which extends over more than 340 acres and is adjoined by Kensington Gardens. Until the Reformation the park belonged to the Manor of Hyde, part of the estates of Westminster Abbey. In late Tudor times it was a royal hunting ground, but James I opened it to the public. The most important event ever to have taken place in Hyde Park was the Great Exhibition of 1851, housed in the Crystal Palace near Rutland Gate. Subsequently the huge structure of glass and iron was taken down and re-erected at Sydenham as a centre of popular entertainment. It was burned down in 1936. On Sundays artists are permitted to display their paintings and drawings in Piccadilly on the railings bordering Green Park (*far right*).

Ci-contre: Buckingham Palace, acheté en 1792 par le roi Georges III est la résidence principale de la famillé royale depuis 1837. Sa façade imposante fait face au boulevard du Mall. Green Park s'étend de St James's Park vers le nord. Le dimanche on permet aux artistes d'exposer leurs peintures en plein air sur les grilles qui séparent le parc de Piccadilly *(ci-dessous, en haut)*. *A gauche et ci-dessous* on voit l'Hôtel Hilton, un des hôtels les plus modernes de Londres.

Ganz links: Buckingham Palace ist seit 1837 die Hauptresidenz der königlichen Familie. Dem Londoner sowie auch dem Ausländer bietet dieser Ort einen besonderen Treffpunkt. Die Anwesenheit der Königin wird der Bevölkerung Londons durch die Fahne über dem Palast angezeigt. *Unten:* Am Sonntag stellen Maler ihre Werke im Green Park aus. Das Hilton Hotel *(links und ganz unten)*, eines der modernsten Hotels von London, überblickt Hyde Park.

The best-known feature of Hyde Park is the large lake called the 'Serpentine' (*above*). It was constructed from pools formed by a little river, the Westbourne, which once flowed through the park. Boating and bathing may be enjoyed here, and an annual regatta attracts a large entry. A bridge of five arches, designed by Rennie, crosses the Serpentine and separates the main part from 'Long Water' in Kensington Gardens.

The principal entrances to the park are at Marble Arch and Hyde Park Corner, both of which are among the busiest traffic junctions in London. At Hyde Park Corner a modern underpass connects Piccadilly with Knightsbridge and has done much to relieve the traffic congestion formerly experienced at this point. The entrance to the park was designed by Burton and erected in 1826. Opposite stands St George's, one of London's most famous hospitals. Part of the eastern fringe of Hyde Park has been taken to provide a double carriageway for Park Lane which leads to the Marble Arch (*lower right*), where a new circulatory traffic scheme has made the Arch the centre-piece of a miniature garden with lawns and ornamental fountains (*upper right*).

From 1828 until 1850 the Marble Arch was situated in front of Buckingham Palace, but the new east front added to the palace by Queen Victoria made it necessary to remove the arch and it was re-erected on its present site in 1851. Near this spot, at the junction of Edgware Road and Oxford Street stood the Tyburn Gallows. The earliest recorded execution here took place in 1196 and the gallows remained in use until the middle of the eighteenth century. Just within the boundary of the park is the enclosed area known as Speaker's Corner, where, within the limits imposed by the law governing public order, anyone may address the curious on any subject, and an audience can usually be guaranteed. Modern offices, flats and a rebuilt cinema in Oxford Street overlook Marble Arch.

Hyde Park, le plus grand des jardins publics de Londres, était terrain de chasse à l'époque Tudor. En 1851 la Grande Exposition eut lieu ici dans le fameux Crystal Palace qui fut démonté pour être reconstruit à Sydenham. *Ci-contre:* La « Serpentine », un lac qui réunit Hyde Park à Kensington Gardens. On peut se baigner ici pendant toute l'année. *Ci-dessous:* Le Marble Arch, à l'extrémité nord du parc, qui se trouvait jadis devant Buckingham Palace. *Ci-dessus:* Des fontaines et un cinéma moderne en face de Marble Arch.

Hyde Park, der grösste Park in London war in der Tudorzeit ein Jagdrevier. Im Jahre 1851 fand hier die Grosse Ausstellung im Kristallpalast statt, der nachher in Sydenham wiederaufgebaut wurde. *Ganz links:* Die „Serpentine", ein schlangenartiger See, verbindet Hyde Park mit Kensington Gardens. *Unten:* Am Nordende von Hyde Park erhebt sich Marble Arch, ein Bogen, der früher vor Buckingham Palace stand. *Oben:* Springbrunnen und ein modernes Kino auf der Nordseite des Parks.

Ci-contre: Kensington Gardens faisait autrefois partie du terrain de Kensington Palace. Ici on peut se retirer du bruit de la circulation pour se reposer ou pour faire des promenades, même en bâteau. La statue de Peter Pan, symbole de la jeunesse éternelle, est à voir ici. *Ci-dessus:* Regents Park situe dans le nord de la capitale, est traversé par le Regent's Canal. Le parc fut disposé par le grand architecte Nash, qui dessina aussi plusieurs rangées classiques qui longent le parc. Une partie de Regents Park est reservée au Jardin Zoologique de Londres qui possède une belle collection d'animaux de tous le coins du monde. Il y a même des jardins sur le toit de quelques grands magasins à Londres. *A droite* on voit le jardin espagnol et (*dessous*) la cour des fontaines, situés sur le toit de Derry and Toms à Kensington.

Ganz rechts: Kensington Gardens bildeten früher einen Teil des Besitzes von Kensington Palace. Im Gegensatz zum Verkehrsgetöse bieten die Gärten Ruhe und Erholung. Hier findet man die schöne Statue von Peter Pan, dem Sinnbild der ewigen Jugend. *Oben:* Regent's Park, der nach Georg dem Vierten genannt ist, ist von dem Regentskanal durchschnitten. Im Sommer fürht man auf der Freilichtbühne beliebte Stücke Shakespeares auf. Ein Teil des Parks bildet den Londoner Zoologischen Garten, wo Tiere aus allen Ländern zu sehen sind. Dachgärten auf Kaufhäusern sind in London keine Seltenheit; unter den schönsten sind diejenigen von Derry and Toms in Kensington. Rechts sieht man den spanischen Garten (*oben*) und den Brunnenhof (*unten*). Hier kann man sich nach anstrengendem Einkaufen ausruhen.

That part of the Serpentine north of Rennie's charming bridge is known as 'Long Water' and is in Kensington Gardens (*above*). The gardens were formerly the private grounds of Kensington Palace and were laid out to the instructions of Queen Caroline, the wife of George II. They contain several delightful features, notably the Flower Walk and the Sunken Garden, while near the 'Long Water' stands the famous statue of Peter Pan by Sir George Frampton. A more forceful piece of sculpture is the bronze cast of Watts' *Physical Energy*, which is situated at the junction of several paths in the centre of the gardens. Kensington Palace was purchased by William III and used as the official royal residence until the end of the reign of George II.

St James's, Green Park, Hyde Park and Kensington Gardens form an almost continuous belt of open country in the heart of London. The other royal parks within the central area are Regent's Park and its northern extension, Primrose Hill. Regent's Park (*far left*) was laid out by Nash in 1811 for the Prince Regent, afterwards George IV. The royal intention of building a palace in the centre of the park was never realised, but the magnificent Classical terraces which border the park give some indication of the grandeur of the whole scheme. There were once a number of private enclosures in the park, but only a few now remain, the others having been absorbed into the park proper. One such is Bedford College for Women, a constituent college of London University. The curiously shaped lake with its islands was formed by damming the course of the little River Tyburn, a tributary of the Thames. There is another lake, a much smaller one, in Queen Mary's Garden within the Inner Circle.

To the majority of people Regent's Park means the 'Zoo' – the menagerie of the Royal Zoological Society, which since 1828 has occupied a triangular area in the northern part of the park. In this comparatively small area there is concentrated one of the most comprehensive collections of animals, birds and reptiles in the world.

Several of London's great stores have laid out gardens on the roofs of their premises. On the left are two views of the 'Spanish Garden' on the roof of Derry and Tom's in Kensington High Street.

The Albert Hall (*below*), the most popular concert hall in London, is a large circular amphitheatre which can accommodate up to 10,000 people. The original intention was that the building should be known as the Royal Albert Hall of Arts and Sciences, and the impetus for its building came from the Prince Consort. The hall, which was opened in 1871, is used for concerts, dances, private and public conventions, and meetings and ceremonies of all kinds. Opposite the hall, in Kensington Gardens, stands the Albert Memorial, erected to the memory of the consort of Queen Victoria and to the Great Exhibition of 1851 with which he was closely connected.

London has a great many museums, many of which are situated in the Borough of Kensington. The Victoria and Albert Museum (*upper right*), opened originally in 1857 and in its present impressive buildings in 1909, has one of the finest collections in the world. Originally it was intended to provide specimens for the study and development of good design, but it outstripped its original aim and has become the comprehensive collection that it is today. The Natural History Museum and the Science and Geological Museums are also in Kensington, but the greatest museum in London, and possibly in the world, is the British Museum in Bloomsbury.

For more than 400 years Chelsea has been fashionable as a residential area, especially among literary and artistic circles. The popularity of Chelsea was at its zenith when Charles II was on the throne, but long before that time many famous people were residents of the borough. In the sixteenth century Sir Thomas More occupied a house near All Saints' Church, and in 1834 Thomas Carlyle made his home in Cheyne Row. Among artists associated with the borough are Turner, Rossetti and Whistler. Cheyne Walk (*lower right*), where Rossetti lived, has some pleasant Georgian houses.

Ci-contre: L'Albert Hall, grand amphithéâtre du 19ᵉ siècle, où ont lieu toutes sortes de concerts. *Ci-dessus:* Le musée Victoria and Albert à Kensington. *Ci-dessous:* Cheyne Walk, dans le quartier résidentiel de Chelsea.

Links: Raum für zehn tausend Personen bietet die Albert Hall, der beliebte Konzertsaal Londons. *Oben:* Das Victoria and Albert Museum. *Unten:* Cheyne Walk, Chelsea, wo einst Rossetti lebte.

Le repère dominant de Battersea, c'est la centrale électrique (*à droite*). Quoiqu'elle ne compte pas parmi les splendeurs d'architecture de la capitale, elle a néanmoins la nuit une certaine attraction théâtrale! *Ci-dessous:* Les jardins d'agrément de Battersea furent construits pour le Festival of Britain en 1951. *Ci-contre:* Kew Gardens, le jardin botanique de Londres, mérite une visite surtout au printemps, quand les fleurs font un beau tableau. Une des particularités plus charmantes du jardin est le lac, bordé d'une avenue appelée Syon Vista.

Rechts: Die Silhouette des Kraftwerks in Battersea während der Abenddämmerung. Obgleich dieses Gebäude nicht zu den Glanzpunkten der Baukunst gehört, besitzt es dennoch eine gewisse theatralische Attraktion. Der Battersea Park liegt am Themseufer zwischen Chelsea Bridge und Albert Bridge. *Unten:* Ein Teil des Parks wurde 1951 für das Festival of Britain als Vergnügungsgarten angelegt. *Ganz rechts:* Kew Gardens, den botanischen Garten Londons sollte man besuchen, vor allem in Frühling, wenn die Blumen am schönsten sind.

The Borough of Battersea lies on the Surrey bank of the Thames opposite Chelsea. Its most conspicuous landmark is the huge power station which can scarcely be counted among the architectural glories of London, although in evening light the silhouette of its tall chimneys, seen through the trees from the north bank of the river (*upper left*), has a curiously theatrical quality. Battersea Park, which extends along the Surrey bank of the Thames between Chelsea and Albert Bridges, covers an area of about 200 acres, including a lake and an Old English Garden. Part of this was set up as an amusement park (*lower left*) for the Festival of Britain in 1951; the park has been retained on a permanent basis and is a popular attraction.

The Royal Botanic Gardens at Kew (*below*) attract thousands of visitors every year, especially in spring, when a multitude of daffodils, crocuses and tulips of every hue make the gardens a glorious sight. Every genus of native plant is to be found here, and many which are not found elsewhere in these islands, for Kew has extensive hot-houses and conservatories. It must not be thought, however, that the gardens are merely a showplace; botanical research is continuously carried out and a great deal of valuable data is published every year. It was at Kew that rubber plants, raised from seeds imported from Brazil, were developed and sent to Malaya to start the great plantations there. In the northern part of the gardens stands Kew Palace, built by a Dutch merchant in the eighteenth century. It was used by George III, and Queen Charlotte died there in 1818. At the other end of the gardens are a Chinese pagoda and a Japanese gateway, the latter modelled on the Buddhist temple. In addition to the Palm and Temperate Houses, the Australian House, the Orangery and several smaller heated buildings, there are three museums and the North Gallery. One of the most attractive features of Kew Gardens is the large lake flanked by an avenue called Syon Vista. From here one can look across the Thames to Syon Park, on the Middlesex shore. Syon House belongs to the Duke of Northumberland. On Kew Green, close to the main entrance of the Gardens, stands the eighteenth-century St Anne's Church, in the churchyard of which is buried the artist Gainsborough.

There are many different characters to be found in the streets of London Town. The coster (*below*), his barrow laden with fruit and vegetables, is frequently to be heard crying his wares in the streets. Sometimes he is accused of causing obstruction, often he is moved on by a sympathetic but firm policeman, but rarely does he lose his habitual cheery demeanour.

London's markets have a fascination for young and old. Many of them are concerned with a particular comestible – Billingsgate for fish, Leadenhall for poultry, Smithfield for meat, and Covent Garden for fruit and vegetables – but there are numerous street markets which have been established for so long that the authority for their existence is often nebulous but seldom questioned. A few are in the West End, but the majority are situated in the City, and none is more popular than the market held in Petticoat Lane (*opposite*), the former name of the thoroughfare now called Middlesex Street in Whitechapel. Here 'bargains' of all kinds appear on the stalls which are set up on Sunday mornings and which disappear as if by magic soon after mid-day.

There are many other characters who help to give London its unique personality. Some who were once a familiar part of the London scene have, alas, almost disappeared. The shoeblack, once a familiar figure, especially in the forecourts of the principal stations, is now seldom to be seen; the lamplighter, with his tall pole, is now only a memory; but others are still with us. The pearly 'kings and queens' who still hold their festivals, and incidentally do a great deal for deserving charities; the porters at Covent Garden who can balance a surprising number of round baskets on their heads; the impassive commissionaires outside hotels, restaurants, cinemas and theatres; the top-hatted bank messengers hurrying busily through the City streets; all these and many more are the real Londoners, without whom the capital would lack its distinctive character.

Ci-dessus: Un marchand des quatre saisons; ces baladeuses se voient souvent dans les rues de Londres. *Ci-contre:* Tous les dimanches un marché en plein vent a lieu dans Middlesex Street, dit « Petticoat Lane ».

Oben: Man begegnet in London einer Reihe typischer Gestalten, wie zum Beispiel dem „Barrow Boy", einem Straßenhändler, der seine Ware ausruft. *Rechts:* Ein Straßenmarkt am Sonntag in „Petticoat Lane".

Ci-dessus, à gauche: Le « bobby », agent de police qui fait l'admiration de tout le monde. *Ci-dessus, à droite:* Un barbouilleur de trottoir. Ces artistes qui travaillent au pastel ont souvent du talent naturel. *A droite:* Les « Chelsea Pensioners » habitent le Royal Hospital à Chelsea, fondé par Charles II. Ces soldats, anciens combattants de l'Armée Britannique, portent une redingote écarlate, uniforme dont ils sont très fier. *Ci-contre:* La Lord Mayor's Show a lieu tous les ans au mois de novembre.

Oben links: Ein ,,Bobby", wie der Londoner Polizist gennant wird, ist nicht nur jeder Verkehrssituation gewachsen, sondern erteilt auch freundlich jede gewünschte Auskunft. *Oben rechts:* Ein Pflastermaler benutzt den Bürgersteig für seine Zeichnungen aus bunter Kreide. *Rechts:* Im Königlichen Hospital von Chelsea wohnen die Veteranen der britischen Armee. In ihrer scharlachroten Uniform sind sie gerngesehene Ehrengäste militärischer Festlichkeiten. *Ganz rechts:* Die Lord Mayor's Show findet jedes Jahr im November statt.

The London 'Bobby' (*far left*), as a policeman is affectionately called, has one of the most responsible jobs in the country. On his shoulders rests the task of coping with every kind of situation – from controlling the complex traffic to preventing a breach of the peace – which may arise at any time in the streets of the capital. His knowledge of London is often encyclopaedic and at any moment he may be approached by visitors seeking information or directions, and his patience and good humour have earned him the respect and admiration of people of all walks of life. Pavement artists (*upper left*) working in crayon on the sidewalks, are still to be found in the streets of London. Their work is often of a high standard and passers-by express their appreciation by throwing coins into the hat.

The lower photograph opposite shows two of the Chelsea Pensioners who are cared for in the Royal Hospital at Chelsea. They wear a distinctive bright scarlet uniform and are often to be seen when they are honoured guests at military functions. Some people would have us believe that Nell Gwynne was responsible for persuading Charles II to found the hospital, but there is little evidence to support this claim. The hospital was certainly founded in the reign of the 'merry monarch' and completed in the reign of William and Mary, and the architect was none other than Sir Christopher Wren whose dignified design is a fitting tribute to those who live there.

One of the most colourful occasions in London is the Lord Mayor's Show which takes place annually in November. The newly elected Lord Mayor proceeds in state in his gilded coach (*below*) to the Law Courts to make a declaration of office, and returns to the Mansion House. The accompanying procession includes a number of decorated floats, usually representative of a particular national theme, as well as detachments of the various services.

All London's docks, with the exception of the Surrey Commercial Docks, are situated on the north bank of the Thames, to the east of Tower Bridge. The Surrey Docks deal chiefly with timber imports. The oldest of the docks is the West India Dock which dates from the very beginning of the nineteenth century; a short time later the London Docks were opened. The largest group, known collectively as the Royal Docks, comprises the Royal Victoria, the Royal Albert and the King George V Docks. The latter, the most modern part of the group, was opened in 1921. The Royal Victoria Dock (*below*), dating from 1855, has been extensively modernised. Further downstream are Tilbury Docks, considerable extensions to which have been carried out. A revolution in the handling of cargo has been taking place during recent years with the development of container traffic. Many consignments which formerly had to be unloaded individually from road or rail transport at the docks and re-loaded on to ships are now enclosed in specially designed containers at the point of origin, and these are speedily transferred at the port with a considerable saving in time and manpower.

Greenwich is famous for its associations with the Royal Navy. In Greenwich are situated the Royal Naval College and the National Maritime Museum. The college occupies the building which was erected at the beginning of the eighteenth century as the Royal Naval Hospital for disabled sailors. In the fifteenth century a royal palace had stood on the same site, and here Henry VIII and his daughters, the future Queens Elizabeth and Mary, were born. The National Maritime Museum occupies the 'Queen's House', a seventeenth-century building designed by Inigo Jones. At Greenwich is preserved the famous old clipper *Cutty Sark* (*opposite*). Sir Francis Chichester's yacht *Gipsy Moth* is berthed near by. The Royal Observatory was formerly situated in Greenwich Park but has now been moved to Herstmonceux in Sussex.

Ci-dessus: Le Royal Victoria Dock, qui date de 1855, forme une partie des Royal Docks, qui s'étendent à l'est de Tower Bridge. *Ci-contre:* A Greenwich se trouve le célèbre clipper *Cutty Sark*.

Oben: Wie fast alle Docks von London befindet sich auch der Royal Victoria Dock am linken Themseufer, östlich der Tower Bridge. *Rechts:* Das berühmte alte Segelschiff „Cutty Sark" ist noch in Greenwich zu sehen.

London Airport, known as Heathrow, was opened in 1946. Although envisaged as one of the most comprehensive airports in the world it soon became evident that it was not large enough, and considerable improvements and additional building have taken place. Nevertheless, it was necessary to construct a second airport at Gatwick which opened in 1958 and replaced the former Croydon airport, and plans have been made for a third airport.

Broadly the passenger airport consists of three main areas. One is devoted to internal flights, to and from destinations within Great Britain and Northern Ireland, the second deals with services within Europe, including Eire, and the third serves passengers for distant destinations. Cargo services are an important part of airline operation, and a new cargo-terminal is nearing completion.

Heathrow is the busiest airport in Europe; twelve million passengers were handled in 1966 and the rate of increase approximates to one million annually. Communication with the centre of London has been improved by the opening of a section of the M4 motorway, and there are plans for a new rail-link with Victoria. The photograph above shows a Trident of British European Airways.

L'aéroport de Londres se trouve à l'ouest de la capitale. C'est l'aéroport le plus mouvementé d'Europe et dessert tous les pays du monde.

Der Londoner Flughafen befindet sich in einer Entfernung von 14 Meilen westlich der Hauptstadt. Er ist der belebteste Europas mit über 12 Millionen Fahrgästen im Jahr.

85306 338 9
© Copyright 1971 Jarrold & Sons Ltd, Norwich
Published and printed in Great Britain by Jarrold & Sons Ltd, Norwich 274